DIARY OF A ROBLOX NOOB

DUNGEON QUEST

BOOK 5
RKID BOOKS

Contents

Noob and Decks: Getting the Swag Back in Dungeon Quest!

Entry # 0.9

Okay, this isn't really the first entry. It does say Entry # 0.9, but... Never mind, I don't need to get into stuff that makes your head spin. Let's start somewhere else instead.

"Watch it, Decks! These sand dudes are pretty tough!"

Decks barely managed to avoid getting his head chopped clean off by one of the sand dudes, who typically wield a wooden longsword. Okay, so it was the most basic weapon in Dungeon Quest, but at least it wasn't a spoon, and it could still do some damage if it connected.

"I've got this, Noob!"

Decks was still surprisingly agile, despite all the bloat from winning a hot-dog-eating competition the day before. He managed to duck under the sword just as the sand dude swung it.

We were outnumbered seven to two. They were relentless. The sand dudes didn't speak— they didn't even have faces. They were just human-looking dudes with arms, bodies, and legs made of sand, but no faces. Pretty creepy if you ask me. Creepy and downright dangerous.

"Take this, you dumb sand moron!" Decks yelled as he took a swing at the nearest one with his bland steel sword, far from the epic purple or legendary gold weapons we had heard about. Blackie the blacksmith from town said that the steel was reinforced, so that made Decks's sword a little sharper. Not much, but enough to count when it hit— enough to turn a sand dude into a sandwich. And this time, Decks would make sure that it did.

Decks swung the sword hard and fast in a fast arc and struck one of the dudes right at his waist, chopping his upper body from his legs. The sand dude's upper half went flying, and that was it for him. I would have felt sorry for him if I didn't know that he and his pals were trying to kill us! Yeah, that's Decks for you. He was terribly out of shape, but he still had a lot of fight and skill left in him. He just couldn't touch his toes if you asked him.

That swing was right on the money, and it actually reminded me of the old Decks. For a moment, he was the death-defying assassin I knew and not the out-of-shape guy that stood in front of me.

"Nice swing, pal! I knew you would get it back!"

"Never lost it, Noob! Now, how about you pitch in and help me take these dudes down?"

Decks asked so nicely, how could I not oblige?

I waved my starter wand in the air a few times, fast enough to whip up two fireballs. That was pretty much the extent of my basic wand's power; beginners don't get much in Roblox.

The two fireballs missed the six remaining sand dudes, but they did strike pretty close to them. Three of them immediately caught on fire. The three dudes started running around like crazy, bumping into their friends and setting them on fire too. Decks pulled out a stick and cooked a marshmallow, which he then ate in one gulp like a hungry pelican.

"Good work, Noob, I think... You set them all on fire, but they're still coming at us!"

I shrugged.

"What can I say? I'm still trying to get the hang of this magic stuff!"

Decks was right. The six sand dudes were still coming at us. If anything, setting them on fire had made them more desperate and dangerous. Well, I couldn't actually tell how they felt since they had no faces. Maybe they were dancing.

One of them took a swing at Decks. Then another. He managed to dodge both swings. Their swords were on fire now, too, and Decks was getting flushed from the heat, even as he moved swiftly to avoid their strikes.

"Whoa, whoa! Those swings were way too close for comfort! I'm getting burned here! Don't you have an ice spell in that wand of yours?"

"Sorry, Decks! It's just a starter wand! It doesn't have much juice!"

"Well, at least you can use it to scratch your butt!"

The sand dudes were getting really close to us now. Being on fire seemed only to have made them nastier. One of them threw a powerful swing at Decks. He managed to raise his sword to defend himself, but the sheer force of the swing knocked it out of his hands.

"Whoa! That's waaay too hot!"

Without his sword, Decks was vulnerable, and I wasn't faring too well myself. I thought maybe I could use my wand like a sword, poke one of the sand dudes in the eye, but—right. No eyes.

One of the sand dudes swung his flaming sword at me. I did the same thing as Decks and raised my starter wand to block his attack, trying to use it as a sword. That was a really bad move. The flimsy wand was no match for the burning steel of the sand dude's sword, and it split like a twig. I immediately screamed like a girl.

Decks and I were both unarmed now and pretty much powerless to do anything. All we could do was slowly back up as the sand dudes closed in on us. I hated sand—it got everywhere—so I didn't even want to imagine what these guys on fire could do!

"Face it, Noob. We're done for. I won't even be able to get my swag back! This whole trip to Dungeon Quest was a failure."

I struggled to think of some smart line, some kind words that could inspire or at least reassure Decks that there was a way out of this. I was thinking of reminding him that he was the world hot-dog-eating champion, but now was not the time to talk about food.

Maybe everything would be all right, but I couldn't think of anything to say. We were doomed.

Or were we?

From out of nowhere, what looked like a huge tank appeared. Was it a tank or a man? I couldn't really be sure at first, it was so huge and intimidating. As it stepped out into the light, I realized the walking tank was actually a man decked out in heavy armor and weapons. It might seem weird that I couldn't tell the different between a tank and a man, but we were in a world fighting sand dudes on fire, so anything was possible. It could have rained chickens next for all we knew.

The armor and weaponry weren't just for show, either—this guy seemed to have the power of a tank as well.

"Okay, that's enough!" he yelled. "None of you sand dudes are getting past me!"

The heavily built man raised his hammer in the air. I recognized it immediately by its purple shimmer. It was an Onyx Hammer, an

Epic weapon. I noticed that the tank dude's equipment was all completely purple–the color of Epic items in Dungeon Quest. This guy was dressed and equipped from head to toe in Epic gear. The only thing that could beat Epic gear was Legendary stuff; our rescuer was clearly a force to be reckoned with.

"You're all going down!"

He slammed his hammer with such force that I thought the whole dungeon would fall down on our heads. It was almost as if a small earthquake was triggered. The ground underneath shook so hard that we could not stand and both of us fell to the ground. There was just no way to stay standing, but our rescuer managed to stay on his feet with no trouble at all. He was a tank, for crying out loud!

"Whoa, Noob! Look at that!"

Decks pointed towards the sand dudes, or

what was left of them. They were not solid anymore. The former sand dudes had been ground to dust by the sheer force of the vibrations on the ground.

"Yeah! Another score for KillGreat!" the tank said.

"KillGreat?" Decks asked.

"I've heard about him. When Blackie gave us background info on this new server, he mentioned KillGreat the Purple Warrior. KillGreat's supposed to be a great warrior who's collected an Epic set for his weapons and armor. A really tough dude."

Decks wasn't listening. He wasn't a very patient guy, and listening to lectures just wasn't his style. He was probably thinking about hot dogs.

"It seems as though my reputation has preceded me. I am KillGreat the Great! Glad to see that you've heard of me!"

"KillGreat the Great? Two 'greats' in one sentence?" I said. "That's kinda wordy, dude."

"You call it wordy, I say it merely emphasizes my being, uh, great. I did want to call myself KillGreat the Most Awesome Warrior Ever, but it didn't sound as... great!"

"I can see that this guy's pretty modest," Decks whispered.

"When I heard that this town had a nasty demon inhabiting its dungeons, I just had to offer my help in taking it down! Blackie the Blacksmith was more than willing to let me try my hand at slaying the demon. He did mention that he sent you both down here before me."

"Well, if that's the case, we're just glad that you showed up when you did, KillGreat. Those dudes were a sand-ful ," I said.

"I don't know. I think we could have handled them easily." I sensed more than a little resentment and jealousy in Decks's voice. He was not as grateful as I was for KillGreat's assistance. By now, I knew Decks well enough to know why he was so bothered by KillGreat.

KillGreat was clearly one of the server's legendary warriors. Blackie had mentioned him, and now that he was right in front of us, we could see for ourselves that he was hot stuff around here. Looking at KillGreat must have reminded Decks of what he once was— before all of the hot dogs. He was reminded of just far he had fallen, and he didn't like it one bit.

"Dream on! It's a miracle someone as large as you can even swing a basic sword!"

Decks's face went red as in response to KillGreat's shocking insult. Decks sucked in his stomach and squared his shoulders.

"Are you making fun of me?"

"And if I am, what are you going to do about it?"

"I could rearrange your face, that's what I could do about it!"

"Oh, please try!"

KillGreat raised his giant hammer with both hands. He looked menacing in his purple armor, like he could take on a thousand sand dudes with no trouble at all. Decks, on the other hand... Let's just say that if I were a betting Noob, I would go for KillGreat in this fight, but I couldn't let it happen. Decks was too angry to see that he would be no match, so I had to step in before Decks got flattened like a pancake.

"Whoa, whoa, whoa! Let's all just take it easy, shall we?" I pleaded. "I mean, there's no need for any violence here. After all, we're all on the same side! We all just want to get to the bottom of this dungeon and take down the demon that's plaguing the town, right?"

I stood between those two warriors; one a

true legend at his peak, and the other a fallen warrior trying to regain his old glory. It was not a very nice position to be in. However, what came next was a lot more unpleasant.

"Watch out!"

It was KillGreat who shouted the warning. He saw the huge fist coming down upon us, and even he was scared! Just in time, we all managed to jump out of the way as the giant fist slammed down, creating several large fractures in the dungeon floor.

"Boy, that would have hurt…" I remarked.

"Well, I don't plan on missing a second time…"

The voice came from above us. We all looked up and saw the huge figure of a sand dude— but much bigger than the others.

We were dealing with some kind of sand giant, and he was really serious about squashing us this time.

Entry #1

The Real Beginning!

Well, enough of all that. We were in a really sticky situation there, but what you're probably wondering is how we ended up in that strange dungeon or even in Dungeon Quest in the first place, right? Well, keep reading and it's going to make sense, I promise!

We had just managed to fight off a wave of ghouls hell-bent on overrunning Mad City. They had been sent by the sinister KingPat to get us at all costs. Luckily, we had Major Creative, a total genius, to help us out!

"All right, guys," Major Creative was saying now. "Here's where we stand. KingPat still wants to get his hands on both of you, and he's willing to destroy anything and anyone that gets in his way!"

"Yeah, Major. We all get that. He almost took down the entire city with those terrible ghoul-things just to get to us. He's nuts!" I said.

"Yeah, nuts and really dangerous. We don't stand a chance against him now, especially considering how out of shape I am!" Decks complained.

He was right. He couldn't stand up to KingPat or any other villain sent to attack us in his current state. I mean, he could make a fantastic human shield, but that was about it.

"Don't be too hard on yourself, Decks. I know it looks bad, but Major Creative will protect us, won't you, Major? You do have your own beef with KingPat!"

Decks perked up at the word beef. Major Creative nodded at us.

"I admit that I did not appreciate KingPat stealing a lot of my old tech and inventions, Noob. You also know from experience that I'm not just going to let something like that just slide. I will get back at him and make him pay."

"See, Decks? We've got the most brilliant mind in all of Roblox on our side!"

"That being said," Major went on, "you do know that old saying about giving a man fish and teaching him how to fish, right?"

I shrugged my shoulders.

"Not really, Major. What does that have to do with anything?"

Major Creative slapped his metal forehead with his metal hand. I could see real frustration on the human side of his face.

"Ugh! You never fail to show me just how intelligent you are, Noob! How someone like you always manages to triumph in so many crazy adventures is beyond me! It just boggles the mind!"

"Hey, you said it yourself, Major! I'm smart! My brains must be the reason why I've always come out on top of my adventures! And what does 'boggled' mean, though?"

Major looked even more frustrated with me.

"I was being sarcastic, Noob! Never mind. I might as well get straight to the point. What I'm saying is, even though I have a lot of amazing tech and inventions to take down KingPat, I will still need both of you to help. Especially you, Decks!"

"Me?"

Decks was clearly surprised.

"Yes, you. You've completely lost your

confidence, and you don't look menacing at all, but you were once one of the deadliest men in Roblox. If we are going to stand a chance taking down KingPat, we will need you back in top shape. We need to bring back the old Decks! We need you to get your swag back!"

"Hey, I know that. That's why I'm training with you. I want to get my swag back too! Right now, I can barely see my feet when I look down."

Major Creative shook his head in frustration.

"We all want you to get your swag back, Decks. And you need to get it now. We need it immediately, ASAP, urgently. With an opponent like KingPat, we can't waste a moment, and your training is just taking too long. That's why we'll need to speed things up a bit. Follow me. Both of you."

"Speed things up? Are we going on a marathon?" asked Decks.

"No!"

"Are we going to the gym?"

"No!"

"Am I allowed to eat hot dogs?"

"Probably, but just follow me, please!"

Major Creative led us both down a long and narrow hallway that wound around like a giant snake. The path led us past places in Major Creative's secret base that we had never seen before.

"Why is there an inflatable castle here?" asked Decks.

"Oh, that, well, it's for training purposes..." said Major.

"Whoa, where are you taking us?" I asked.

"Be patient, Noob. I'm taking you both to one of my greatest inventions. It's so great that I've kept it a secret. Until now."

Finally, the hallway came to an end, and we stepped into a large room full of computers and equipment. Nothing new for a genius inventor like Major Creative. What was new sat in the center of the room. There was a wide platform with just enough room for two people to stand on.

"Both of you, stand on that platform."

We both did as we were told. Major went over to one of the computers and began pressing buttons. Decks and I had no idea what he was doing, but with Major, it was sure to be anything but dull, that was for certain.

"What now? What do you want us to do?"

"What are you doing?"

"You both have so many questions. Let me just get to the point. You're both standing on a working time machine!" Major said proudly.

Both Decks and I were shocked. Major Creative

was a genius, there was no doubt about that. But could he really have created a machine that could go back and forth through time?

"Major, are you serious?"

"I'm very serious, Noob! I told you it was my greatest invention!"

"Wait a minute here!" Decks said. "If this is the actual time machine, why are we standing on it?"

Major Creative smiled at us. It really was his best invention since the umbrella for dogs.

"You're a lot smarter than you look, Decks. Yes, you're both standing on the time machine. Remember what I said earlier? We need you to get back into shape as fast as possible so you can help take down KingPat. Well, this time machine is the way to do just that!"

"To do what? Get me back in shape? I don't understand, Major Creative. How is a time machine going to get me back in shape?"

"Pretty simple! I've set the coordinates for the distant past. A time when Roblox was an even more dangerous place than it is now. I've set the coordinates to take you both to… Dungeon Quest!"

Decks and I froze in horror. In the Dungeon Quest era, warriors fought endlessly in long maze-like dungeons, taking down infinite numbers of monsters and enemies. It was known for swords, magic, and endless battles. This was scary, but I could see Major Creative's point; forced to fight for his life for days or weeks on end, Decks would surely get his swag back. If he survived.

"Wait a second here! You're going to toss us into Dungeon Quest? How are we going to get back? And what if we don't want to go?" I demanded.

"I will be monitoring you both, Noob. When I

see that you and Decks are both stronger for it, especially Decks, then I will bring you both back here in a flash. And if you don't want to go? Well, sorry, you don't really have a choice now."

Decks was furious, and I couldn't blame him, but it was too late. The platform glowed under our feet, and there was a loud humming noise. Everything suddenly became bright. This would be heaven to a giant human moth! It was so bright I thought I might go blind. In all the confusion, I hugged Decks.

"What the…?"

As we were swallowed up by the light, we heard Major speak one last time.

"See you both in Dungeon Quest! Have fun!"

Entry #2

The World of Dungeon Quest!

When the bright lights finally faded, Decks and I cautiously stepped down from the platform. Well, it was more like the platform vanished from beneath us. Decks and I screamed as we landed on our feet.

I looked around. The lights were gone, and we were clearly not at the base anymore. Instead, we were standing outside among woods and rolling hills. This was not the base, but this definitely wasn't Mad City either.

Decks was fuming, but there really wasn't anything either of us could do. It was clear that we were far away from Major Creative now. I wanted to cheer Decks up, so I started to line dance. He normally loved my silly dance moves, but this time, it had no effect.

"Wow," I said. "He really did take us thousands of years into Roblox's past and into Dungeon Quest! Look around. We're clearly not at the base anymore!"

Decks nodded.

"We're outside and definitely nowhere in the city, that much is certain. Still, that's no guarantee that he actually did manage to send us back in time! Maybe he just invented a fancy teleporter and teleported us out into the countryside."

Decks did have a point. Nothing had yet proven we had gone back in time. Still, I knew from past experiences that Major Creative rarely made any blunders, especially when it came to his inventions. Well, except for that one time he turned Decks into a pickle, but that was an accident. A delicious one.

"Give us your valuables, travelers! Give 'em all up or we'll lop your bald heads off your shoulders!"

The two bandits came out of nowhere. I guess they must have been hiding in the bushes just waiting to rob some unfortunate travelers passing by. Or maybe my dancing had attracted them. I noticed that they were wearing weird, outdated clothes. They also carried daggers, not guns. All our doubts vanished.

Being robbed was pretty scary, but it was what they had said that got Decks's and my attention.

"Bald? I am bald! You're bald, too, Noob! What's going on here?"

Decks felt his bare scalp. He had never been

bald before. I did the same thing and noticed that I was bald too.

"Maybe it's a side-effect from the time travel?" Decks guessed. "Or maybe it's because we're in Dungeon Quest? I read up on this period in Roblox history. The greatest warriors of this time were always bald when they had no armor on. Either way, it looks like Major did it. Major Creative really did send us back in time!"

The two bandits growled at us. They didn't like us talking to each other. Or maybe they didn't like bald people.

"What are you two babbling about? Have you both gone insane?" one said.

"Maybe they've both had a little too much ale to drink, eh? They're talking nonsense!"

"Whatever! It doesn't matter. Just give us all your belongings, or we'll gut you where you stand!"

When Decks heard the bandits' threat, he snapped. It was almost as if some invisible switch had been flipped inside of him. He turned red and suddenly flew into a wild rage. He charged at the two men like a wild boar. The two bandits didn't know what had hit them; one minute they were standing, and the next, they were knocked off their feet.

"Nobody guts me! Nobody! I'm Decks, the greatest assassin in Roblox! Do you hear me? I'm Decks!"

As Decks spoke, he stomped on one of the bandits lying on the ground. The other staggered to his feet and attempted to tackle Decks, but it wasn't going to happen. Decks simply wouldn't fall.

"I can't knock him over! He's too fat!" one shouted.

"What did you just say?"

Apparently, this bandit wasn't smart. It was

already clear that Decks was more than a little sensitive. Still, the bandit just had to run his mouth, and he paid dearly for it. Decks began to pound him as he lay on the ground, battering him over and over again with his fists. Truth be told, I was getting a little scared here, and not for Decks. I was getting worried for the bandit.

"That's enough, Decks! He's had enough!"

Decks wouldn't listen and just kept on beating the poor dude. I had no choice but to pull him off the helpless bandit before anything else happened. Believe me, that wasn't easy without a forklift.

"That's enough, Decks! You clearly beat them both already!"

"Sorry, Noob. I just couldn't help myself. Man, I could really use a soda."

"I know what you mean, Decks, but you've got to keep your head on your shoulders. It's clear that we are in Dungeon Quest now, and we've got to find a way back to our own time. I promise you, once we get out of here, I will get you a soda. A diet one…"

"Bravo! Bravo!"

The unfamiliar voice came from behind us. Decks and I turned around, ready for any potential threat. Instead, we came upon an old man with a belly that was almost as round as Decks's. He clapped his hands, clearly pleased to see us.

"Who are you?" Decks asked.

"I am Blackie the Blacksmith. I was just passing by when I saw you take down those bandits. Truth be told, I was actually worried I would be robbed by them before you showed up! They've been plaguing this road for quite some time now, don't you know? In fact, they've robbed so many travelers that there is a bounty on their heads! You and your friend are the only ones who have managed to stop them; you've both done a great service for my town."

I was flattered that the traveler mentioned me in the same breath as Decks, but I simply couldn't take the credit here.

"Thanks, but honestly, my friend Decks here did all the work. You saw what happened for yourself."

"My friend is just too modest," Decks said. "I couldn't have done it without him! You mentioned a bounty for these two losers? Well, Noob and I would be happy to collect it!"

"And you will get it, mighty warrior Decks, but now that I am here, I must also ask another favor of you and your friend, Noob."

"Go on..."

"Our town has a little demon problem..."

Okay, any sentence with the two words

"demon" and "problem" in it did not sound good at all.

"You see," the old man continued, "our town is being plagued by a demon known as the Sand Giant."

"Sand Giant? That sounds really scary."

"Scary doesn't even begin to describe the Sand Giant, Noob. The Sand Giant had long been vanquished by the old warriors of our realm. It was only recently that he respawned in the deepest parts of our underground dungeon. He especially hates bald people and kittens!"

"This monster must be really evil if he doesn't like kittens! How do you know he respawned if the dungeon is underground?" I asked.

"Simple. The Sand Giant is accompanied by all manner of bad luck and tragic events. Recently, our town has been under attack by many foul creatures. These bandits were just two of them."

"They're not even creatures. They're bandits."

Blackie ignored me and kept speaking.

"They have arrived because of the bad luck that the Sand Giant brings. The only way to stop all the bad luck and the monsters invading the town is to defeat the Sand Giant in battle."

"I can see where this is headed, and I don't like it," I muttered.

"Let me get this straight. You want us both to go down into your underground dungeon and destroy this Sand Giant? Am I right?"

Decks hit the nail on the head. Blackie nodded immediately.

"That is exactly what I want you to do. It's not just for me. It's for the entire town. And we will reward you generously for your efforts. A lot of Robux await you after you defeat the Sand Giant—a lot more than the bounty for these bandits."

"Sounds good to me!"

Decks was more than eager to get started. That was Decks for you. I was a lot more cautious and more reluctant to trust Blackie.

"Whoa, maybe we ought to think this through before agreeing to anything, Decks!"

"What's the matter, Noob? Don't tell me you're afraid to take down a sand demon?"

"Yes, I am afraid, Decks, and there's nothing wrong with that! Listen to what you just said— we're supposed to take down a sand demon! We don't even know what that is!"

Decks shrugged. There was not even a hint of worry on his face.

"What are you so concerned about? So it's a big, bad Sand Giant. So we've never seen or faced anything like that before. So what? If these bandits came from the Sand Giant, he can't be too bad himself, right?"

That didn't sound right at all, but Decks was so sure of himself that he refused to listen. I couldn't help but worry.

"I don't know, Decks. I still think that we should be really careful about this…"

"If you don't want to go chasing after the Sand Giant, what else do you propose we do? You saw how I took down those bandits earlier, right? For a moment, I was the old Decks again; dangerous, strong, and not to be messed with! For just one moment, I had my swag back! If we take down this Sand Giant, just think! Major Creative might just bring us back home."

Now that Decks put it that way, it all made a lot more sense. We had been sent back in time for Decks to get his swag back. That was all that really mattered now. Seeing him take down those petty crooks had reminded me of the old Decks. I had seen flashes of his old moves and confidence, and if he kept this up, I was sure he would get stronger in no time at all. And knowing Major Creative, I was sure that he was somehow keeping tabs on us. He could probably see everything that was going on and was waiting for the right moment to bring us back to our own time.

"All right, Decks. I guess you're right. Let's do this then."

"There! I knew you would see it my way! You need some warriors to take down your Sand Giant, Blackie? Well, Noob and I are your boys! We'll get the job done for you!"

"Wonderful! Follow me! I've got some extra horses you both can use. They mostly just carry supplies for us back in town, but they're sturdy animals. I used to travel by cow, but they stop every three minutes to poop, so I got horses. I'm sure they won't mind carrying you, Noob, and those two dastardly bandits back to town. Once we get there, I'll provide you with some weapons and gear that you can use against the Sand Giant!"

It all sounded good, and with that, we rode off with Blackie towards the town. Our adventure in Dungeon Quest had just begun.

Entry #3

Down Into the Dungeons.

The first thing we did once we reached town was deposit the two bandits at the jail. The town jail was horrific, full of criminals. It was scary when they smiled their toothless grins.

 There were a lot of other bandits and weird creatures already jamming the cells. Many of the creatures looked a lot more dangerous than the bandits.

"Glad that you took care of those two. They don't look much, but they're a lot more dangerous than they seem," the warden said.

The warden had a beard so long that you could use it as a jump rope.

"I don't get it, warden," I said. "The Sand Giant is in the town's underground dungeon? Isn't *that* supposed to be where you keep prisoners?"

"Not really, Noob. Those underground dungeons were built thousands of years ago. They were basically abandoned until the Sand Giant reared his ugly head and spawned there. You'll find nothing but danger and trouble down there."

"Just how I like it!" Boy, Decks was really getting confident. He seemed ready to fight anyone.

I really wished that I shared his confidence, but I didn't. Honestly, I was scared of what we would face once we went underground. There could be anything there; monsters, bandits, a bear with a shark's head that shot lasers.

"You've got a really confident one here, Blackie," the warden said.

"I'm confident in Decks, and Noob, too, warden! You should have seen how Decks took out those two bandits!"

I just hoped that Decks and I were worthy of that faith.

The warden didn't look so confident, and that made me even more worried than I already was. The prisoners in the cells were not making things any easier for us, either, especially when they smiled at us with toothless grins. It was like looking at a bunch of evil grannies! They shouted at us through the bars.

"Two more warriors to send down the dungeon? The master demon will eat them alive, just like he did the ones before!"

"Yeah! Don't you guys get tired of sending

poor losers to their doom? It's getting really pathetic! The Sand Giant's going to have your heads!"

"Eat us alive? Have our heads? Decks, this doesn't sound like a good idea at all!"

"Don't let them get to you, Noob. We can handle this silly demon! Besides, if you ever chicken out, I'll be there to save your butt."

"There you go! Good money for easy work, don't you think?" Blackie was just as upbeat as Decks, but that was likely because *he* wasn't going to fight the Sand Giant.

"You got it! I can't wait to get my hands on that Sand Giant! I'll take him down personally!"

"Patience, Decks. You'll get your shot. One thing at a time. Now that we've deposited those two losers in the town jail and paid you both handsomely, it's time to equip you with the weapons and gear that will take down the Sand Giant! You're both going to become legends!"

I didn't mention it, but legends usually became legends only *after* they kicked the bucket. But there was no point in showing how scared I already was. We were here now, and we had to defeat the Sand Giant.

"Okay, boys. Follow me to my workshop."

Blackie led us out of the jail. I could see that he took a lot of pride in his workshop and all the weapons there, and for good reason.

"All right! Look at all this stuff! I know I can take down the giant now!" Decks said.

Blackie beamed with pride as we browsed through the weapons.

"Yep. I crafted all those weapons myself. Worked my hands to the bone to create such fine beginner and novice weapons."

"Wait… beginner and novice weapons?"

"Yes, Noob. All I can craft are the starting weapons for your journey. The really powerful weapons are gained through conquering monsters. That's why it's called a dungeon grind, right? You have to grind to get the good stuff!"

So we would be facing a potentially endless parade of monsters armed with only the most basic of weapons. That was really reassuring, all right! We might as well be given some bananas to fight with.

"Well, what are you two waiting for? Take your pick already!"

Decks took a long steel sword. It looked pretty boring, but I guess it was reliable.

"I'll go for this long sword. Looks really sharp and powerful."

"The colorless steel sword! Bland but effective. I think it's a wonderful choice," Blackie affirmed.

I took a look at all the weapons around me. Most of them looked too heavy for a dude like myself. A small wand in the corner of Blackie's workshop caught my eye. It shimmered with some kind of energy.

"I think I'll take that wand," I said. I hadn't had much experience with wands, but I was willing to give it a whirl.

"The starter wand. It's got basic magical energies coursing through it. Good for a few fireballs here and there, and great for the starting magician or wizard."

I took the wand and waved it in the air. Suddenly, everything started to get hot, and before I knew what was happening, a small fireball shot out of the end of the wand. It almost struck Decks and Blackie, who only just managed to dive out of the way in time. The fireball exploded on the stone floor, sparking a small blaze.

"Be careful how you swing that wand around! It's really sensitive!"

Blackie used a pail of water to quickly douse the flames.

"Sorry about that," I said.

"Never mind. Anyway, why don't you both wear some armor to complement your weapons? You would be sitting ducks entering that dungeon without anything on your bald heads. Try my novice armor on! It should help. Not by much, but a little at least!"

"Not by much?" I asked warily.

"Oh, don't mind me! Just put it on, already! Better that than no protection at all, right?"

Decks didn't seem to be worried in the slightest. If anything, putting on the novice armor seemed to pump him up even further. I was hoping to find a wig for my bald head, but Blackie had none.

"Look at me! I'm a warrior! I'm going to get my swag back in no time at all! Come on, Noob! Let's go take down that Sand Giant and get this all over with."

Blackie pointed to a hatch in the middle of the town square. I could smell it from where I stood, and it was horrible, like fresh poop. "I'm sure you'll both do just fine. Just open that hatch, and the underground dungeon awaits!"

Without further ado, Decks ran over to the hatch and forced it open. There was absolutely no fear in him as he climbed down into the darkness. I followed close behind, not knowing what to expect. I just hoped that Decks could get his swag back quickly so that we could get out of here as soon as possible.

Entry #4

Getting the Swag Back

And that, in a nutshell, is how Decks and I ended up taking on a giant Sand Giant with KillGreat.

The three of us were staring up at the nasty-looking monster. Unlike the other sand dudes, this giant could talk, and he was not happy.

"You guys killed Mort, Abner, Josh, Bill, Willie, Tony, and Curt! I'm going to squash you for killing them!"

"Whoa, you memorized those sand dudes'

names?"

My remark only seemed to anger the Sand Giant further. It seemed so strange—the sand dudes had no faces, so how would the Sand Giant know who was who? And the sand dudes had been so mean, who would want to be friends with them? Maybe they all built sand castles together.

"They were my best buds! Now you're all going to pay!"

"That's our cue to get out of the way!" Decks shouted.

The Sand Giant took another swing at us with his closed fist. The three of us managed to dive aside in time, but this was getting really tiresome, and fast.

"We can't keep doing this! Sooner or later, he's going to connect with one of those fists of his!" I called.

"I agree! We have to end this right—"

Before KillGreat could even finish his sentence, the Sand Giant took a wicked swing at him with his giant arm.

He swatted KillGreat away with his open palm like some kind of giant fly swatter. The effect was devastating as poor KillGreat went flying through the air.

"Yeow! That must have really hurt! Is KillGreat still in one piece?" I asked.

"I wouldn't worry too much, Noob! He's decked out in Epic Gear. It should be able to withstand a blow like that. Besides, I don't really care if he's out of it or not, to be honest. I don't like him!"

The Sand Giant took another swing. I managed to dodge it once more, but it turned out the giant wasn't really trying to swat or squash me. Instead, catching me off guard, he hammered his fist on the ground. The vibrations were so powerful that I was knocked on my butt. It hurt like crazy.

"Pretty smart, eh?" the monster roared with a laugh. "Now that you're flat on your butt, you're going down for sure!"

The Sand Giant was gloating, and why not? Nailing me with a fake swing that I never saw coming *was* a smart move. I figured that this was it. After so many adventures in Roblox, now was the time for me to finally meet my end, squashed by a Sand Giant in an ancient server.

"Hey, Sandy! I wouldn't be too sure of that!"

Just as I thought I was done for, I heard a familiar voice coming from behind the Sand Giant. The demon turned and was shocked to see Decks running towards him. The monster was so focused on squashing me that he hadn't even noticed Decks slipping away. Now, Decks was almost on top of him. And he was holding

KillGreat's hammer.

I don't know how Decks managed to do it, but he jumped into the air and raised the heavy hammer up over his head. He landed on the Sand Giant's head and brought down the full weight of the Onyx hammer on the hapless demon's skull.

"Eat this, jumbo sand dude!"

From the ground where I was watching, it looked painful. That was one powerful blow that fell upon the Sand Giant's head. There was a flash of light as the hammer made impact, and I heard the giant cry out in pain.

After that, there was nothing but silence. The Sand Giant was gone, and in his place, there was nothing but a whole lot of sand. Decks stood triumphantly, still holding the Onyx hammer.

"Scratch out one Sand Giant," he said proudly.

"Decks, that was... that was awesome."

What else could I say? I couldn't believe just how easily Decks had taken the Sand Giant, and with such a heavy weapon too! Awesome was just one word to describe it; it was amazing, incredible, fantastic, and everything else in between.

Decks swelled with pride, and he smiled from ear to ear.

"Well, I was just being myself, and..."

"...and I think you got your swag back."

"You really mean that, Noob? For real?"

"Hey, man, I don't know how else you can describe a guy who took down a Sand Giant all by himself..."

Decks began a little victory dance, shaking his butt around. It looked like a lot of fun, and I started to dance too.

"Hey! I think you've got something that's mine!"

We both stopped dancing with our butts and turned around to see KillGreat. He was on rubbery legs, but he was still standing and was just about managing to walk. I guess that purple Epic armor of his was just as tough as I had expected it to be.

"That Onyx hammer is mine, and I want it back now!"

KillGreat was still in one piece, and he was *mad.*

"Decks, uh, it's all over," I said. "The sand dudes are done for. Maybe you should just do as he says and..."

"Try and take it, you big loser!"

Maybe it was because he was still pumped up from taking down the Sand Giant. Or maybe it was because he didn't like KillGreat very much.

Or maybe it was just because he was still Decks the assassin, someone who wouldn't hesitate to steal or kill if it suited his needs. Either way, Decks said it, and the challenge was on.

"Oh, I'm taking it, all right, even if I have to pry it out of your dead hands!"

"Bring it on!"

This was not good. This was not good at all. I tried to deescalate the situation by line dancing—maybe they would both laugh at my silly antics—but my line dancing failed for the second time that day.

Entry #5

The Way of Nature

"Decks, come on. We don't need to get into a fight with this guy…"

I stepped in front of Decks in the hope of stopping him. Of course, that didn't do much, especially now that he had gotten his swag back.

"Get out of the way!"

Decks swung the hammer and knocked me aside. With all the power that the Onyx hammer had, it was a minor miracle that Decks didn't take off my head. I guess he held back because I was his friend. Or at least I hoped so.

Decks was eager for a fight with KillGreat, and KillGreat was willing to oblige. I couldn't believe it. Why did Decks have to pick *now* of all times to get into a fight? And with an Epic warrior to boot!

KillGreat charged at Decks, and Decks charged back fearlessly. That was Decks for you— totally reckless. Yep, his swag was really coming back now.

"I'll kill you!"

KillGreat was roaring with fury now.

"Not if I squash you with your own hammer first!"

Like two runaway trains headed for a collision on the same track, they continued to run towards each other. There was nothing I could do but lie on the ground and watch the titanic battle unfold.

"Come on, Major! You must be watching from somewhere, monitoring all this! If you are, get us out of this server already before Decks gets himself killed!"

It was useless. I might as well have been pleading to the wind. If Major Creative was monitoring this situation, which I was certain he was, he was not getting us out of there. No, Decks would have to finish this pointless fight that he'd started.

Decks tried to do the same thing to KillGreat as he had to the Sand Giant. Raising the hammer as he jumped into the air, he aimed for KillGreat's head, using even more force than before.

Unfortunately for him, KillGreat was not the Sand Giant. This time, his opponent was not going to just stand around waiting to get pulverized. Despite being decked out in armor, KillGreat could move surprisingly fast. He managed to jump out of the way just as Decks threw down the hammer, hitting the floor with an almighty boom.

"That should have been your head! Stand still so I can chop you down to size!"

Decks swung the hammer hard, but it was a wild swing, and KillGreat easily ducked.

"You're going to have to be a lot faster than that if you want to hit me with my own hammer!" KillGreat sneered and taunted Decks by shaking his butt in the air.

"Blast you! Stay still and I'll do more than just hit you; I'll squish you like a bug!"

Decks took several more wild swings, missing KillGreat each time. I could see what KillGreat was trying to do, and it was working brilliantly. Decks was exhausted. I could tell by his labored breathing and slowing movements. The hammer seemed to be getting heavier and heavier for Decks now, and it was showing.

"Stay still, blast you!"

"Not for you, I won't!"

That's when it happened. Decks was so tired now that he was an easy target for KillGreat. He didn't even need an Epic weapon to take him down. KillGreat threw a nasty uppercut, struck him flush on the chin, and sent him flying. He fell to the ground, dropping KillGreat's hammer in the process.

KillGreat reached for his hammer and stood over Decks, who was unarmed and completely helpless.

"Now, you're going to pay for even trying to take my hammer!"

"No! Don't kill him!"

I had to do something! I couldn't just stand there and watch as KillGreat crush Decks. Sure, he was a former assassin, probably wasn't all there, and definitely wasn't the nicest person around, but we had shared a considerable amount of time and adventures together already. I couldn't just let him get killed like this.

KillGreat turned towards me and laughed. He clearly didn't see me as a threat. In fact, he laughed so hard that it was insulting.

"Yeah? How are *you* going to stop me from killing him?"

Good question. I was pretty much helpless, and I didn't stand a chance against a seasoned warrior like KillGreat. Or did I?

I looked at the ground and noticed a long wooden staff. It looked like any ordinary staff, except for the markings on it. Looking more closely, I realized that the markings were actually an inscription.

"Whoever is worthy may use the power of the DooDoo staff."

I had no idea what the inscription meant. Sounded like a weapon for Decks—he loved to poop.

It seems crazy, but it was almost as if I wasn't acting alone, like some strange energy was guiding my actions. I took the staff and raised it above my head, slamming it down to the ground just as KillGreat was about to pound Decks's head with his hammer.

As the DooDoo staff hit the ground, there was a blinding light.

"That light! I can't see!"

"Noob, what did you do?"

When the light faded, we found ourselves in a different location entirely. There was snow and ice everywhere, and it was freezing.

"Where are we? It's so blasted cold, I can barely move!" Decks said.

"For once I agree with you, Decks. Where is

this place, and what sorcery has brought us here?"

"You have been summoned to the true, final area of the underground dungeon, Epic warrior KillGreat! Here, you and your friends will perish!"

"Who said that? What's going on?"

We turned around to see what appeared to an Ice Wizard. He was flanked by several guards, each one made entirely of ice.

"You've all made it this far thanks to the power of the DooDoo staff! But this is where your journey must end," the Ice Wizard said.

KillGreat stared at me in a mixture of awe and disbelief. He could not believe what he was hearing. "The DooDoo staff? You found and used the DooDoo staff? Impossible!"

"Believe it! Your friend there found the lost DooDoo staff; apparently, he is the one true worthy user of its magical powers. Only the DooDoo staff has enough power to transport anyone directly to the last level of the dungeon. And here is where the true menace is: the Ice Elemental!"

"The Ice Elemental? I don't get it! I thought that the Sand Giant was the big problem!" Decks questioned.

Decks was right. We were all confused here. What was going on? The Ice Wizard smiled as a giant made solely of ice walked up behind him and his ice minions. This giant was a lot larger than the one made of sand and looked a whole lot more menacing.

"The Sand Giant was indeed the first menace. It spawned in the dungeon after waiting patiently for thousands of years. Once it came out, the monsters all followed. Unfortunately, one of the monsters that it spawned was our boss, the Ice Elemental. And you know how it is with sand and ice. Freeze sand and it turns to ice, which is pretty brittle and easy to smash..."

"So you're saying this is some kind of hostile takeover? One of the lesser dudes takes over the spot of the big dog?" Decks queried.

The Ice Wizard grinned.

"Exactly. The Sand Demon's time was up. The better and stronger monster had to take over. It's simply the way of things. In nature, the stronger, younger wolves take over leadership of the pack. Out with the old and in with the new. This is exactly how it should be."

Decks looked pleased.

"Great. I didn't want this to be too easy."

KillGreat turned and actually smiled at Decks as he helped him to his feet. It took great effort. I thought Decks would have to roll from side to side like a tortoise to get back on his feet.

It seemed they weren't fighting any longer.

"Perhaps I misjudged you. Perhaps you're a true warrior after all."

Decks nodded at KillGreat.

"Likewise, KillGreat. Now, how about we take all these ice monsters down and save the town?"

"Let's go!"

The three of us charged towards the Ice Wizard, his horde of ice minions, and the Ice Elemental looming behind them. Yeah, it was going to be a tough fight, all right.

Entry #6

The Chosen One

So there we all were. Me, Decks, and KillGreat versus the Ice Wizard, his ice minions, and the real threat, the Ice Elemental, standing like a great shadow behind them.

"Take them all down!"

"Show no mercy!"

Decks and KillGreat charged right in with no fear or hesitation. I ran right behind them.

That strange energy from earlier suddenly

began to control me, and it was coming from the DooDoo staff. I had no idea how to use this thing, but I was suddenly waving it around like a pro. It was strange, but it was almost as if the staff and I were connected somehow.

I waved the DooDoo staff above my head, and streams of fire shot out towards our enemies. The fire radiated from the end of the staff, striking several of the ice minions before they could even touch us. They melted instantly.

I could hear the panic in the chatter of the ice minions, and so could KillGreat and Decks.

Inspired by the DooDoo causing so much damage, KillGreat and Decks charged through the minions, slicing and dicing as they went. The ice minions all quickly fell to the Onyx hammer and Decks's own recently returned swag. We were making them into ice cubes with ease.

"They're taking us down! We don't stand a

chance!"

The Ice Wizard was panicking. There was no way we could lose now, was there?

"Fool! Their power is only as good as that DooDoo staff! Get rid of it, and we take them all out!" The Ice Elemental barked the order at the Ice Wizard, who promptly went to work.

A powerful blast sent icicles shooting up from the ground beneath my feet. Pain hit me all over my body, and I fell to the ground, dropping the DooDoo staff.

"Noob! They got Noob!" I heard Decks shout as the ice blast nailed me hard. There was clear shock in his voice, but there was nothing he could do now. His voice sounded like a distant echo.

"He's dropped the DooDoo staff! That was the only thing that could take us down! This is our chance! The Ice Elemental has commanded it, and victory will be ours!" I heard some ice dude say.

The events that followed remain a bit of a blur. I was knocked so hard to the ground that I could barely stay awake, much less understand what was going on. That Ice Wizard really packed a punch, and I was down for the count.

I could barely keep my eyes open, but what I did see was, well, awful. The ice minions began to overwhelm KillGreat and Decks. They were both fighting valiantly, though. Decks took down three ice minions as they charged at him, and from what I could see, KillGreat took down ten of them, an amazing feat in itself. But despite their best efforts, the ice minions just kept on coming.

"They're swarming all over us! We've got to keep on fighting!" Decks shouted.

"Fight on! Don't stop! We can still take them!" KillGreat responded.

It was a nice thought, but it was not very likely.

The odds quickly stacked against us once I went down.

KillGreat and Decks fought as hard as they could, but the ice minions were now all over them, and there was not much they could do.

I could hear the distant sound of the Ice Wizard gloating as I lay on the ground. Decks and KillGreat had disappeared under a pile of ice minions who were beating them senseless. I could barely stand up, let alone help, and all really did seem lost.

But that was when Decks did the unthinkable. I don't know how he did it, but Decks managed to break free from the ice minions that were holding him down. It was only for a few moments, but it was all the time that he needed.

"Catch that pig! He's trying something!"

The ice minions chased after Decks, but he was too fast. He ran to the DooDoo staff and managed to reach it before they did.

"I don't know how to use this magic thing! All I know is that you can use it, Noob. So use it!"

Decks tossed the DooDoo staff my way, just as the ice minions finally overwhelmed him.

"Catch, Noob! And do your thing!"

I was still dizzy and barely conscious, but I had to move. I couldn't just lie there, not after Decks's valiant move. I gathered what little strength I had left and stretched out my hand. I'm not even sure if I was the one that moved, or if it was the magic energy from the DooDoo staff that gave me the strength to reach out and catch it, but suddenly its magical powers were back in my grasp.

"No!" the Ice Elemental cried. He was afraid for good reason. I was going to destroy them for calling Decks a pig. Only I can call him that.

The magic energy from the staff started

to power me, and I felt the strength in my body returning. I was connected to this staff somehow, and I was not going to fail. I raised it up in the air, and it began to fire huge bursts of flame at the Ice Wizard and his minions, melting several of them right where they stood.

Most of the ice minions were melted now, and Decks and KillGreat were free.

"Your friend is amazing with the DooDoo staff!" remarked KillGreat. "The prophecy said that whoever was able to wield the DooDoo staff would come from another time and place. I think your friend is the chosen one!"

"No! I won't allow it! I won't allow you to defeat me, not when I'm so close to total victory!" the Ice Elemental whined. "I took down the Sand Giant! I won't be defeated by some Noob!"

He was the only cold dude now remaining. He

stalked towards me, and I admit that I was terrified. I mean who wouldn't be scared of a huge, angry ice giant? Shutting my eyes tightly, I pointed the DooDoo staff in his direction and let its powers take over.

The staff fired a powerful bolt, and the Ice Elemental walked right into it. We had been freezing the whole time we had been there, but when that bolt hit the Ice Elemental, it felt as if we were all in volcano. We instantly started sweating in our armor.

"No! No! No!" the Ice Elemental protested, but there was nothing he could do now. The firebolt hit him right in the middle of his chilly body, and he began to melt. We watched as his legs started to turn to liquid, then his chest and arms, and finally his head. The Ice Elemental was like a giant scoop of melting ice cream.

"No... it can't... be... it..."

It was all over for him now.

A few moments later it was done. There was nothing left of the mighty Ice Elemental but a puddle of water. It was truly over.

"We did it! We did it! The Ice Elemental has been defeated!" I cheered.

I wanted to jump for joy, and I could tell that KillGreat and Decks were just as happy.

"Let's face it, you did most of the work, Noob. We couldn't have defeated all those ice minions if it weren't for you and that staff," Decks said.

"I agree with Decks. You have proven yourself to be a great warrior today, Noob. You are the chosen one. Songs will be sung about you, and people will remember you as a hero," KillGreat said.

I was starting to blush. They were both laying it on me thick.

RKID Books

"You're both too modest, you know that? I couldn't have done anything without your help. I don't even know how to use this thing!" I admitted.

"You used it perfectly today, and that's what counts," Decks said. "Take it from me, Noob. You'll learn how to use that thing in time. I saw how you handled it. You were a natural. You and that thing are meant for each other. We came here to get my swag back, but it seems as if we got something even more important, and that's you discovering your own swag! KillGreat's right; you've been chosen by something much higher."

I paused and thought about what Decks had said. He wasn't one to give compliments freely or think about deep stuff, so he must have really meant all of it. I still wasn't sure what was going on here, but I realized that I now had a weapon of my own and a power we could use against KingPat. Decks was right.

That was really something amazing.

Right after he spoke, a bright light flashed, and when it cleared a platform had appeared—the same platform that had brought us here to Dungeon Quest!

"It's the time machine! Major Creative really must have been watching us all along!" I said.

"Yeah, I guess he's pretty satisfied that I've got my swag back, and you've got a snazzy new staff and cool magical powers! I can't blame him; even I would be pleased with those developments."

It was time for a victory dance. We all started shaking our butts in the air, and we didn't care if Major Creative was watching. Perhaps he was dancing, too, wherever he was.

"Well, I guess this is goodbye, KillGreat. It's been a pleasure fighting by your side and shaking butts," Decks said.

"Yeah, you too, Decks. I didn't like you at first, but it turns out you're okay!"

KillGreat shook our hands.

"If this is the magic device that sent you here, well, goodbye it is. Take care! I will remember you both very fondly."

With that, Decks and I stepped onto the platform to head home. Our adventure was over, but we still had a long way to go.

If you enjoyed this book, please leave a review on Amazon! It would really help me with the series.

Best,

RKID Books

The Story Continues...

https://geni.us/srs2

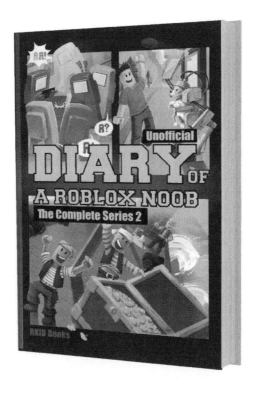

Printed in Great Britain
by Amazon

79267122R00052